50 Baking with Alternative Flavors Recipes for Home

By: Kelly Johnson

Table of Contents

- Almond Flour Chocolate Chip Cookies
- Coconut Flour Banana Bread
- Quinoa Flour Brownies
- Oat Flour Pancakes
- Chickpea Flour Muffins
- Gluten-Free Lemon Bars
- Cassava Flour Pizza Crust
- Rice Flour Chocolate Cake
- Almond Butter Cookies
- Flaxseed Meal Bread
- Sweet Potato Pie with Almond Crust
- Avocado Chocolate Mousse
- Coconut Macaroons
- Maple Syrup Oatmeal Cookies
- Buckwheat Flour Pancakes
- Chia Seed Pudding Cake
- Pumpkin Spice Muffins with Coconut Flour
- Teff Flour Brownies
- Hazelnut Chocolate Spread Cookies
- Beetroot Brownies
- Almond Milk Banana Muffins
- Cashew Butter Chocolate Chip Cookies
- Gluten-Free Cinnamon Rolls
- Zucchini Bread with Coconut Flour
- Carrot Cake with Almond Flour
- Dairy-Free Chocolate Cupcakes
- Spelt Flour Chocolate Chip Cookies
- Vegan Pumpkin Bread
- Millet Flour Banana Bread
- Coconut Oil Chocolate Cake
- Peanut Butter and Jelly Cookies
- Flax Egg Pancakes
- Raw Vegan Cheesecake
- Chocolate Chip Chickpea Blondies
- Cornmeal Muffins

- Tapioca Flour Cookies
- Coconut Flour Snickerdoodles
- Almond Milk Scones
- Lentil Flour Brownies
- Sweet Potato Muffins with Oat Flour
- Gluten-Free Chocolate Torte
- Carob Flour Cookies
- Green Banana Flour Pancakes
- Vegan Coconut Macaroons
- Oat and Honey Granola Bars
- Quinoa Chocolate Chip Cookies
- Brown Rice Flour Cookies
- Acorn Flour Pancakes
- Vegan Blueberry Muffins
- Chocolate Avocado Cake

Almond Flour Chocolate Chip Cookies

Ingredients

- 2 cups almond flour
- 1/2 teaspoon baking soda
- 1/4 teaspoon salt
- 1/3 cup coconut oil or unsalted butter, melted
- 1/2 cup brown sugar (or coconut sugar)
- 1/4 cup granulated sugar
- 1 teaspoon vanilla extract
- 1 large egg
- 1 cup chocolate chips (semi-sweet or dark)

Instructions

1. **Preheat the Oven:** Preheat your oven to 350°F (175°C) and line a baking sheet with parchment paper.
2. **Mix Dry Ingredients:** In a medium bowl, whisk together the almond flour, baking soda, and salt until well combined.
3. **Combine Wet Ingredients:** In a large bowl, mix the melted coconut oil (or butter), brown sugar, and granulated sugar until smooth. Add the vanilla extract and egg, mixing until fully incorporated.
4. **Combine Mixtures:** Gradually add the dry ingredients to the wet ingredients, stirring until a dough forms. Fold in the chocolate chips.
5. **Shape the Cookies:** Scoop tablespoon-sized portions of dough and place them onto the prepared baking sheet, spacing them about 2 inches apart. Flatten them slightly, as they won't spread much during baking.
6. **Bake:** Bake for 10-12 minutes or until the edges are golden brown. The centers may look slightly underbaked; they will firm up as they cool.
7. **Cool:** Let the cookies cool on the baking sheet for about 5 minutes before transferring them to a wire rack to cool completely.
8. **Enjoy:** Serve warm or store in an airtight container for up to a week.

These almond flour chocolate chip cookies are chewy and flavorful, perfect for satisfying your sweet tooth! Enjoy baking!

Coconut Flour Banana Bread

Ingredients

- 1/2 cup coconut flour
- 3 ripe bananas, mashed
- 4 large eggs
- 1/3 cup honey or maple syrup
- 1/4 cup coconut oil, melted
- 1 teaspoon vanilla extract
- 1/2 teaspoon baking soda
- 1/2 teaspoon baking powder
- 1/4 teaspoon salt
- 1 teaspoon cinnamon (optional)

Instructions

1. **Preheat the Oven:** Preheat your oven to 350°F (175°C) and grease a loaf pan or line it with parchment paper.
2. **Mix Wet Ingredients:** In a large bowl, combine the mashed bananas, eggs, honey (or maple syrup), melted coconut oil, and vanilla extract. Mix until well combined.
3. **Add Dry Ingredients:** In another bowl, whisk together the coconut flour, baking soda, baking powder, salt, and cinnamon (if using).
4. **Combine Mixtures:** Gradually add the dry ingredients to the wet ingredients, stirring until a thick batter forms. Let it sit for about 5 minutes to allow the coconut flour to absorb moisture.
5. **Bake:** Pour the batter into the prepared loaf pan and smooth the top. Bake for 45-55 minutes, or until a toothpick inserted into the center comes out clean.
6. **Cool:** Allow the banana bread to cool in the pan for 10 minutes before transferring it to a wire rack to cool completely.
7. **Enjoy:** Slice and serve as a delicious breakfast or snack!

Quinoa Flour Brownies

Ingredients

- 1 cup quinoa flour
- 1/2 cup cocoa powder
- 1/2 teaspoon baking powder
- 1/4 teaspoon salt
- 1/2 cup coconut oil or unsalted butter, melted
- 1 cup brown sugar (or coconut sugar)
- 2 large eggs
- 1 teaspoon vanilla extract
- 1/2 cup chocolate chips (optional)

Instructions

1. **Preheat the Oven:** Preheat your oven to 350°F (175°C) and grease an 8x8-inch baking pan or line it with parchment paper.
2. **Mix Dry Ingredients:** In a bowl, whisk together the quinoa flour, cocoa powder, baking powder, and salt until well combined.
3. **Combine Wet Ingredients:** In another bowl, mix the melted coconut oil (or butter), brown sugar, eggs, and vanilla extract until smooth.
4. **Combine Mixtures:** Gradually add the dry ingredients to the wet ingredients, stirring until fully combined. Fold in chocolate chips if using.
5. **Bake:** Pour the batter into the prepared baking pan and spread it evenly. Bake for 20-25 minutes, or until a toothpick inserted into the center comes out mostly clean.
6. **Cool:** Allow the brownies to cool in the pan for about 10 minutes before transferring them to a wire rack to cool completely.
7. **Enjoy:** Cut into squares and serve as a rich, gluten-free treat!

Oat Flour Pancakes

Ingredients

- 1 cup oat flour
- 1 tablespoon baking powder
- 1/2 teaspoon salt
- 1 tablespoon sugar (optional)
- 1 cup milk (or dairy-free alternative)
- 1 large egg
- 2 tablespoons melted butter or coconut oil
- 1 teaspoon vanilla extract

Instructions

1. **Mix Dry Ingredients:** In a bowl, whisk together the oat flour, baking powder, salt, and sugar (if using).
2. **Combine Wet Ingredients:** In another bowl, combine the milk, egg, melted butter (or coconut oil), and vanilla extract. Whisk until smooth.
3. **Combine Mixtures:** Pour the wet ingredients into the dry ingredients and stir until just combined. Let the batter rest for about 5 minutes.
4. **Preheat the Pan:** Heat a non-stick skillet or griddle over medium heat and lightly grease it.
5. **Cook Pancakes:** Pour 1/4 cup of batter onto the skillet for each pancake. Cook until bubbles form on the surface (about 2-3 minutes), then flip and cook for another 1-2 minutes until golden brown.
6. **Serve:** Serve warm with your favorite toppings, such as maple syrup, fruit, or yogurt.

Enjoy making and tasting these delicious recipes!

Chickpea Flour Muffins

Ingredients

- 1 cup chickpea flour
- 1/2 teaspoon baking powder
- 1/4 teaspoon salt
- 1/2 teaspoon cumin (optional)
- 1/4 teaspoon black pepper (optional)
- 1/2 cup water (or as needed)
- 1/4 cup olive oil
- 1 tablespoon maple syrup (optional)
- 1/4 cup chopped vegetables (bell peppers, spinach, etc.)

Instructions

1. **Preheat the Oven:** Preheat your oven to 350°F (175°C) and grease a muffin tin or line it with muffin liners.
2. **Mix Dry Ingredients:** In a bowl, whisk together the chickpea flour, baking powder, salt, cumin, and black pepper.
3. **Combine Wet Ingredients:** In another bowl, mix the water, olive oil, and maple syrup until combined.
4. **Combine Mixtures:** Add the wet ingredients to the dry ingredients, stirring until a batter forms. Fold in the chopped vegetables.
5. **Bake:** Divide the batter evenly among the muffin cups and bake for 20-25 minutes, or until a toothpick inserted into the center comes out clean.
6. **Cool and Serve:** Allow the muffins to cool for a few minutes before removing them from the tin. Enjoy warm or at room temperature!

Gluten-Free Lemon Bars

Ingredients

- 1 cup almond flour
- 1/4 cup coconut oil, melted
- 1/4 cup honey or maple syrup
- 1/4 teaspoon salt
- 3 large eggs
- 1/2 cup fresh lemon juice
- 1/4 cup honey or maple syrup (for filling)
- 1 teaspoon lemon zest
- 1/4 teaspoon baking powder

Instructions

1. **Preheat the Oven:** Preheat your oven to 350°F (175°C) and line an 8x8-inch baking dish with parchment paper.
2. **Make the Crust:** In a bowl, mix the almond flour, melted coconut oil, honey (or maple syrup), and salt until crumbly. Press this mixture into the bottom of the prepared dish.
3. **Bake the Crust:** Bake the crust for 10-12 minutes, or until lightly golden.
4. **Prepare the Filling:** In a bowl, whisk together the eggs, lemon juice, honey (or maple syrup), lemon zest, and baking powder until smooth.
5. **Bake Again:** Pour the filling over the baked crust and return to the oven for an additional 20-25 minutes, or until the filling is set.
6. **Cool and Serve:** Allow to cool before slicing into bars. Dust with powdered sugar if desired and enjoy!

Cassava Flour Pizza Crust

Ingredients

- 1 1/2 cups cassava flour
- 1 teaspoon baking powder
- 1/4 teaspoon salt
- 1/2 cup water (or as needed)
- 1 tablespoon olive oil

Instructions

1. **Preheat the Oven:** Preheat your oven to 425°F (220°C) and line a baking sheet with parchment paper.
2. **Mix Dry Ingredients:** In a bowl, combine the cassava flour, baking powder, and salt.
3. **Add Wet Ingredients:** Gradually add water and olive oil, mixing until a dough forms. It should be pliable but not sticky.
4. **Shape the Crust:** Transfer the dough to the prepared baking sheet and press it out into a round shape, about 1/4 inch thick.
5. **Pre-bake:** Bake the crust for 15-20 minutes until lightly golden.
6. **Add Toppings and Finish Baking:** Add your favorite pizza toppings and bake for an additional 10-15 minutes. Enjoy your gluten-free pizza!

Rice Flour Chocolate Cake

Ingredients

- 1 cup rice flour
- 1/2 cup cocoa powder
- 1 teaspoon baking powder
- 1/2 teaspoon baking soda
- 1/4 teaspoon salt
- 1/2 cup sugar
- 1/2 cup vegetable oil
- 2 large eggs
- 1 teaspoon vanilla extract
- 1 cup milk (or dairy-free alternative)

Instructions

1. **Preheat the Oven:** Preheat your oven to 350°F (175°C) and grease an 8-inch round cake pan.
2. **Mix Dry Ingredients:** In a bowl, whisk together the rice flour, cocoa powder, baking powder, baking soda, salt, and sugar.
3. **Combine Wet Ingredients:** In another bowl, mix the vegetable oil, eggs, vanilla extract, and milk until smooth.
4. **Combine Mixtures:** Gradually add the wet ingredients to the dry ingredients, stirring until combined.
5. **Bake:** Pour the batter into the prepared cake pan and bake for 25-30 minutes, or until a toothpick inserted in the center comes out clean.
6. **Cool and Serve:** Allow the cake to cool in the pan for 10 minutes before transferring it to a wire rack. Serve as a delightful dessert!

Almond Butter Cookies

Ingredients

- 1 cup almond butter
- 1/2 cup coconut sugar (or brown sugar)
- 1 large egg
- 1 teaspoon vanilla extract
- 1/2 teaspoon baking soda
- 1/4 teaspoon salt

Instructions

1. **Preheat the Oven:** Preheat your oven to 350°F (175°C) and line a baking sheet with parchment paper.
2. **Mix Ingredients:** In a bowl, combine the almond butter, coconut sugar, egg, vanilla extract, baking soda, and salt. Mix until a dough forms.
3. **Shape Cookies:** Scoop tablespoon-sized portions of dough and place them on the prepared baking sheet, spacing them about 2 inches apart. Flatten them slightly.
4. **Bake:** Bake for 10-12 minutes or until the edges are golden.
5. **Cool and Enjoy:** Allow the cookies to cool on the baking sheet for a few minutes before transferring them to a wire rack.

Flaxseed Meal Bread

Ingredients

- 1 cup flaxseed meal
- 1/2 cup almond flour
- 1/2 teaspoon baking powder
- 1/4 teaspoon salt
- 1/4 cup water
- 2 large eggs
- 1 tablespoon olive oil

Instructions

1. **Preheat the Oven:** Preheat your oven to 350°F (175°C) and grease a small loaf pan.
2. **Mix Dry Ingredients:** In a bowl, combine the flaxseed meal, almond flour, baking powder, and salt.
3. **Combine Wet Ingredients:** In another bowl, whisk together the water, eggs, and olive oil.
4. **Combine Mixtures:** Add the wet ingredients to the dry ingredients and mix until a dough forms.
5. **Bake:** Pour the mixture into the prepared loaf pan and bake for 30-35 minutes, or until a toothpick inserted in the center comes out clean.
6. **Cool and Slice:** Allow to cool before slicing. Enjoy as a gluten-free bread option!

Sweet Potato Pie with Almond Crust

Ingredients

For the Almond Crust:

- 1 1/2 cups almond flour
- 1/4 cup coconut oil, melted
- 2 tablespoons honey or maple syrup
- 1/4 teaspoon salt

For the Filling:

- 1 1/2 cups cooked sweet potato, mashed
- 1/2 cup coconut milk
- 1/4 cup honey or maple syrup
- 2 large eggs
- 1 teaspoon vanilla extract
- 1 teaspoon cinnamon
- 1/4 teaspoon nutmeg (optional)

Instructions

1. **Preheat the Oven:** Preheat your oven to 350°F (175°C) and grease a pie pan.
2. **Make the Crust:** In a bowl, mix the almond flour, melted coconut oil, honey (or maple syrup), and salt until crumbly. Press the mixture into the bottom and up the sides of the prepared pie pan.
3. **Pre-bake the Crust:** Bake the crust for 10-12 minutes until lightly golden.
4. **Prepare the Filling:** In a bowl, mix the mashed sweet potato, coconut milk, honey (or maple syrup), eggs, vanilla extract, cinnamon, and nutmeg until smooth.
5. **Assemble and Bake:** Pour the filling into the pre-baked crust and smooth the top. Bake for an additional 30-35 minutes, or until the filling is set.
6. **Cool and Serve:** Allow to cool before slicing. Serve as a delicious dessert!

Avocado Chocolate Mousse

Ingredients

- 2 ripe avocados
- 1/4 cup cocoa powder
- 1/4 cup maple syrup (or honey)
- 1/4 cup almond milk (or dairy-free alternative)
- 1 teaspoon vanilla extract
- Pinch of salt

Instructions

1. **Blend Ingredients:** In a food processor, combine the avocados, cocoa powder, maple syrup (or honey), almond milk, vanilla extract, and salt. Blend until smooth and creamy.
2. **Adjust Sweetness:** Taste and adjust sweetness as desired by adding more maple syrup (or honey).
3. **Chill:** Transfer the mousse to serving bowls and refrigerate for at least 30 minutes to set.
4. **Serve:** Serve chilled, garnished with fresh berries or nuts if desired. Enjoy this rich and creamy dessert!

Enjoy making and tasting these delicious recipes!

Coconut Macaroons

Ingredients

- 2 1/2 cups shredded coconut (unsweetened)
- 1/2 cup sweetened condensed milk
- 1 teaspoon vanilla extract
- 1/4 teaspoon salt
- 2 large egg whites

Instructions

1. **Preheat the Oven:** Preheat your oven to 325°F (160°C) and line a baking sheet with parchment paper.
2. **Mix Ingredients:** In a large bowl, combine the shredded coconut, sweetened condensed milk, vanilla extract, and salt. Mix well.
3. **Whip Egg Whites:** In another bowl, beat the egg whites until stiff peaks form. Gently fold the whipped egg whites into the coconut mixture until just combined.
4. **Shape Macaroons:** Using a cookie scoop or your hands, form small mounds of the mixture and place them on the prepared baking sheet.
5. **Bake:** Bake for 20-25 minutes or until the macaroons are golden brown on the edges.
6. **Cool and Serve:** Allow to cool on the baking sheet for a few minutes before transferring to a wire rack. Enjoy as a sweet treat!

Maple Syrup Oatmeal Cookies

Ingredients

- 1 cup rolled oats
- 1 cup almond flour
- 1/2 teaspoon baking soda
- 1/2 teaspoon salt
- 1/2 cup coconut oil, melted
- 1/2 cup maple syrup
- 1 teaspoon vanilla extract
- 1/2 cup chocolate chips or raisins (optional)

Instructions

1. **Preheat the Oven:** Preheat your oven to 350°F (175°C) and line a baking sheet with parchment paper.
2. **Mix Dry Ingredients:** In a bowl, combine the rolled oats, almond flour, baking soda, and salt.
3. **Combine Wet Ingredients:** In another bowl, mix the melted coconut oil, maple syrup, and vanilla extract until smooth.
4. **Combine Mixtures:** Gradually add the wet ingredients to the dry ingredients and stir until combined. Fold in chocolate chips or raisins if using.
5. **Shape Cookies:** Drop tablespoon-sized portions of dough onto the prepared baking sheet, spacing them about 2 inches apart.
6. **Bake:** Bake for 12-15 minutes or until the edges are golden.
7. **Cool and Enjoy:** Allow to cool on the baking sheet for a few minutes before transferring to a wire rack.

Buckwheat Flour Pancakes

Ingredients

- 1 cup buckwheat flour
- 1 tablespoon baking powder
- 1/4 teaspoon salt
- 1 tablespoon sugar (optional)
- 1 cup milk (or dairy-free alternative)
- 1 large egg
- 2 tablespoons melted butter or coconut oil
- 1 teaspoon vanilla extract

Instructions

1. **Mix Dry Ingredients:** In a bowl, whisk together the buckwheat flour, baking powder, salt, and sugar (if using).
2. **Combine Wet Ingredients:** In another bowl, combine the milk, egg, melted butter (or coconut oil), and vanilla extract. Whisk until smooth.
3. **Combine Mixtures:** Pour the wet ingredients into the dry ingredients and stir until just combined. Let the batter rest for about 5 minutes.
4. **Preheat the Pan:** Heat a non-stick skillet over medium heat and lightly grease it.
5. **Cook Pancakes:** Pour 1/4 cup of batter onto the skillet for each pancake. Cook until bubbles form on the surface (about 2-3 minutes), then flip and cook for another 1-2 minutes until golden brown.
6. **Serve:** Serve warm with your favorite toppings like syrup, fruit, or yogurt.

Chia Seed Pudding Cake

Ingredients

- 1/2 cup chia seeds
- 2 cups almond milk (or dairy-free alternative)
- 1/4 cup maple syrup (or honey)
- 1 teaspoon vanilla extract
- 1/2 teaspoon cinnamon (optional)
- 1 cup almond flour (for the cake layer)
- 1 teaspoon baking powder

Instructions

1. **Prepare Chia Pudding:** In a bowl, combine chia seeds, almond milk, maple syrup, vanilla extract, and cinnamon (if using). Stir well and let sit for about 15 minutes to thicken.
2. **Preheat the Oven:** Preheat your oven to 350°F (175°C) and grease a small baking dish.
3. **Make the Cake Layer:** In another bowl, mix almond flour and baking powder. Gradually add the thickened chia pudding to the almond flour mixture and stir until combined.
4. **Bake:** Pour the batter into the prepared baking dish and bake for 25-30 minutes, or until set.
5. **Cool and Serve:** Allow to cool before slicing. Serve as a unique dessert or breakfast treat!

Pumpkin Spice Muffins with Coconut Flour

Ingredients

- 1 cup coconut flour
- 1/2 cup pumpkin puree
- 3 large eggs
- 1/4 cup honey or maple syrup
- 1/4 cup coconut oil, melted
- 1 teaspoon vanilla extract
- 1 teaspoon baking soda
- 1 teaspoon pumpkin pie spice
- 1/4 teaspoon salt

Instructions

1. **Preheat the Oven:** Preheat your oven to 350°F (175°C) and line a muffin tin with paper liners.
2. **Mix Wet Ingredients:** In a large bowl, combine pumpkin puree, eggs, honey (or maple syrup), melted coconut oil, and vanilla extract. Mix until smooth.
3. **Mix Dry Ingredients:** In another bowl, whisk together the coconut flour, baking soda, pumpkin pie spice, and salt.
4. **Combine Mixtures:** Gradually add the dry ingredients to the wet ingredients, stirring until well combined.
5. **Fill Muffin Tin:** Divide the batter evenly among the muffin cups.
6. **Bake:** Bake for 20-25 minutes, or until a toothpick inserted in the center comes out clean.
7. **Cool and Enjoy:** Allow to cool before serving. Enjoy these flavorful muffins!

Teff Flour Brownies

Ingredients

- 1 cup teff flour
- 1/2 cup cocoa powder
- 1/2 teaspoon baking powder
- 1/4 teaspoon salt
- 1/2 cup coconut oil or unsalted butter, melted
- 1 cup brown sugar (or coconut sugar)
- 2 large eggs
- 1 teaspoon vanilla extract
- 1/2 cup chocolate chips (optional)

Instructions

1. **Preheat the Oven:** Preheat your oven to 350°F (175°C) and grease an 8x8-inch baking pan or line it with parchment paper.
2. **Mix Dry Ingredients:** In a bowl, whisk together the teff flour, cocoa powder, baking powder, and salt.
3. **Combine Wet Ingredients:** In another bowl, mix the melted coconut oil (or butter), brown sugar, eggs, and vanilla extract until smooth.
4. **Combine Mixtures:** Gradually add the dry ingredients to the wet ingredients, stirring until fully combined. Fold in chocolate chips if using.
5. **Bake:** Pour the batter into the prepared baking pan and spread it evenly. Bake for 20-25 minutes or until a toothpick inserted in the center comes out mostly clean.
6. **Cool and Serve:** Allow to cool before cutting into squares. Enjoy as a delicious dessert!

Enjoy making and tasting these delightful recipes!

Hazelnut Chocolate Spread Cookies

Ingredients

- 1 cup almond flour
- 1/2 cup hazelnut flour
- 1/4 cup cocoa powder
- 1/4 teaspoon baking soda
- 1/4 teaspoon salt
- 1/4 cup coconut oil, melted
- 1/4 cup maple syrup
- 1 teaspoon vanilla extract
- 1/2 cup hazelnut chocolate spread

Instructions

1. **Preheat the Oven:** Preheat your oven to 350°F (175°C) and line a baking sheet with parchment paper.
2. **Mix Dry Ingredients:** In a bowl, whisk together the almond flour, hazelnut flour, cocoa powder, baking soda, and salt.
3. **Combine Wet Ingredients:** In another bowl, mix the melted coconut oil, maple syrup, and vanilla extract until smooth.
4. **Combine Mixtures:** Add the wet ingredients to the dry ingredients and mix until well combined.
5. **Shape Cookies:** Scoop tablespoon-sized portions of dough and place them on the prepared baking sheet. Make a small indentation in the center of each cookie and fill it with hazelnut chocolate spread.
6. **Bake:** Bake for 12-15 minutes or until the edges are set.
7. **Cool and Serve:** Allow to cool on the baking sheet for a few minutes before transferring to a wire rack.

Beetroot Brownies

Ingredients

- 1 cup cooked and pureed beetroot
- 1/2 cup almond flour
- 1/2 cup cocoa powder
- 1/4 cup maple syrup or honey
- 1/4 cup coconut oil, melted
- 2 large eggs
- 1 teaspoon vanilla extract
- 1/2 teaspoon baking powder
- 1/4 teaspoon salt

Instructions

1. **Preheat the Oven:** Preheat your oven to 350°F (175°C) and grease an 8x8-inch baking pan or line it with parchment paper.
2. **Mix Wet Ingredients:** In a bowl, combine the beetroot puree, almond flour, cocoa powder, maple syrup (or honey), melted coconut oil, eggs, and vanilla extract. Mix until smooth.
3. **Add Dry Ingredients:** Stir in the baking powder and salt until well combined.
4. **Bake:** Pour the batter into the prepared baking pan and spread it evenly. Bake for 25-30 minutes or until a toothpick inserted in the center comes out mostly clean.
5. **Cool and Serve:** Allow to cool before cutting into squares. Enjoy these fudgy brownies!

Almond Milk Banana Muffins

Ingredients

- 1 cup almond flour
- 1 cup mashed ripe bananas (about 2-3 bananas)
- 1/4 cup almond milk
- 2 large eggs
- 1/4 cup honey or maple syrup
- 1 teaspoon baking powder
- 1/2 teaspoon baking soda
- 1/2 teaspoon cinnamon (optional)
- 1/4 teaspoon salt

Instructions

1. **Preheat the Oven:** Preheat your oven to 350°F (175°C) and line a muffin tin with paper liners.
2. **Mix Wet Ingredients:** In a large bowl, combine the mashed bananas, almond milk, eggs, and honey (or maple syrup) until well combined.
3. **Mix Dry Ingredients:** In another bowl, whisk together the almond flour, baking powder, baking soda, cinnamon (if using), and salt.
4. **Combine Mixtures:** Add the dry ingredients to the wet ingredients and stir until just combined.
5. **Fill Muffin Tin:** Divide the batter evenly among the muffin cups.
6. **Bake:** Bake for 18-20 minutes or until a toothpick inserted in the center comes out clean.
7. **Cool and Enjoy:** Allow to cool before serving. Enjoy these moist muffins!

Cashew Butter Chocolate Chip Cookies

Ingredients

- 1 cup cashew butter
- 1/2 cup coconut sugar
- 1/2 teaspoon baking soda
- 1/4 teaspoon salt
- 1 large egg
- 1 teaspoon vanilla extract
- 1/2 cup chocolate chips

Instructions

1. **Preheat the Oven:** Preheat your oven to 350°F (175°C) and line a baking sheet with parchment paper.
2. **Mix Ingredients:** In a bowl, combine the cashew butter, coconut sugar, baking soda, salt, egg, and vanilla extract. Mix until smooth.
3. **Fold in Chocolate Chips:** Gently fold in the chocolate chips.
4. **Shape Cookies:** Scoop tablespoon-sized portions of dough and place them on the prepared baking sheet, spacing them about 2 inches apart.
5. **Bake:** Bake for 10-12 minutes or until the edges are lightly golden.
6. **Cool and Serve:** Allow to cool on the baking sheet for a few minutes before transferring to a wire rack.

Gluten-Free Cinnamon Rolls

Ingredients

- 2 cups almond flour
- 1/2 cup coconut flour
- 1/4 cup honey or maple syrup
- 1/4 cup coconut oil, melted
- 3 large eggs
- 1 tablespoon cinnamon
- 1/4 teaspoon salt
- 1 teaspoon baking powder

Instructions

1. **Preheat the Oven:** Preheat your oven to 350°F (175°C) and grease a baking dish.
2. **Mix Dry Ingredients:** In a bowl, whisk together almond flour, coconut flour, cinnamon, salt, and baking powder.
3. **Combine Wet Ingredients:** In another bowl, mix the honey (or maple syrup), melted coconut oil, and eggs until smooth.
4. **Combine Mixtures:** Gradually add the dry ingredients to the wet ingredients and mix until a dough forms.
5. **Roll Out Dough:** Place the dough between two pieces of parchment paper and roll it out into a rectangle. Sprinkle with cinnamon and additional sweetener if desired.
6. **Roll and Slice:** Roll the dough tightly into a log and slice it into rolls. Place them in the greased baking dish.
7. **Bake:** Bake for 25-30 minutes or until lightly golden.
8. **Cool and Serve:** Allow to cool before serving. Enjoy these warm cinnamon rolls!

Zucchini Bread with Coconut Flour

Ingredients

- 1 cup grated zucchini (squeeze out excess moisture)
- 1/2 cup coconut flour
- 1/4 cup honey or maple syrup
- 3 large eggs
- 1/4 cup coconut oil, melted
- 1 teaspoon vanilla extract
- 1/2 teaspoon baking soda
- 1/4 teaspoon salt
- 1 teaspoon cinnamon (optional)

Instructions

1. **Preheat the Oven:** Preheat your oven to 350°F (175°C) and grease a loaf pan.
2. **Mix Wet Ingredients:** In a large bowl, combine the grated zucchini, coconut flour, honey (or maple syrup), eggs, melted coconut oil, and vanilla extract. Mix until well combined.
3. **Add Dry Ingredients:** Stir in the baking soda, salt, and cinnamon (if using) until just combined.
4. **Pour into Loaf Pan:** Pour the batter into the prepared loaf pan and smooth the top.
5. **Bake:** Bake for 30-35 minutes or until a toothpick inserted in the center comes out clean.
6. **Cool and Serve:** Allow to cool before slicing. Enjoy this moist zucchini bread!

Carrot Cake with Almond Flour

Ingredients

- 2 cups almond flour
- 1/2 cup shredded carrots
- 1/4 cup honey or maple syrup
- 3 large eggs
- 1/4 cup coconut oil, melted
- 1 teaspoon vanilla extract
- 1 teaspoon baking powder
- 1 teaspoon cinnamon
- 1/4 teaspoon salt

Instructions

1. **Preheat the Oven:** Preheat your oven to 350°F (175°C) and grease a round cake pan.
2. **Mix Wet Ingredients:** In a bowl, combine the shredded carrots, honey (or maple syrup), eggs, melted coconut oil, and vanilla extract. Mix well.
3. **Mix Dry Ingredients:** In another bowl, whisk together the almond flour, baking powder, cinnamon, and salt.
4. **Combine Mixtures:** Gradually add the dry ingredients to the wet ingredients and mix until well combined.
5. **Pour into Cake Pan:** Pour the batter into the prepared cake pan and smooth the top.
6. **Bake:** Bake for 25-30 minutes or until a toothpick inserted in the center comes out clean.
7. **Cool and Serve:** Allow to cool before serving. Enjoy this delicious carrot cake!

Enjoy making and tasting these delightful recipes!

Dairy-Free Chocolate Cupcakes

Ingredients

- 1 cup all-purpose flour
- 1/2 cup cocoa powder
- 1/2 cup coconut sugar or brown sugar
- 1/2 teaspoon baking soda
- 1/2 teaspoon baking powder
- 1/4 teaspoon salt
- 1 cup almond milk or any dairy-free milk
- 1/4 cup coconut oil, melted
- 1 teaspoon vanilla extract
- 1 tablespoon apple cider vinegar

Instructions

1. **Preheat the Oven:** Preheat your oven to 350°F (175°C) and line a cupcake tin with paper liners.
2. **Mix Dry Ingredients:** In a bowl, whisk together the flour, cocoa powder, coconut sugar, baking soda, baking powder, and salt.
3. **Combine Wet Ingredients:** In another bowl, mix the almond milk, melted coconut oil, vanilla extract, and apple cider vinegar until smooth.
4. **Combine Mixtures:** Add the wet ingredients to the dry ingredients and stir until just combined.
5. **Fill Cupcake Liners:** Pour the batter into the lined cupcake tins, filling each about 2/3 full.
6. **Bake:** Bake for 18-20 minutes or until a toothpick inserted in the center comes out clean.
7. **Cool and Serve:** Allow to cool before frosting or serving.

Spelt Flour Chocolate Chip Cookies

Ingredients

- 1 cup spelt flour
- 1/2 teaspoon baking soda
- 1/4 teaspoon salt
- 1/2 cup coconut sugar or brown sugar
- 1/4 cup coconut oil, melted
- 1/4 cup almond milk
- 1 teaspoon vanilla extract
- 1/2 cup chocolate chips

Instructions

1. **Preheat the Oven:** Preheat your oven to 350°F (175°C) and line a baking sheet with parchment paper.
2. **Mix Dry Ingredients:** In a bowl, whisk together the spelt flour, baking soda, and salt.
3. **Combine Wet Ingredients:** In another bowl, mix the coconut sugar, melted coconut oil, almond milk, and vanilla extract until smooth.
4. **Combine Mixtures:** Add the wet ingredients to the dry ingredients and mix until just combined. Fold in the chocolate chips.
5. **Shape Cookies:** Scoop tablespoon-sized portions of dough and place them on the prepared baking sheet.
6. **Bake:** Bake for 10-12 minutes or until the edges are lightly golden.
7. **Cool and Serve:** Allow to cool on the baking sheet for a few minutes before transferring to a wire rack.

Vegan Pumpkin Bread

Ingredients

- 1 1/2 cups all-purpose flour
- 1 cup canned pumpkin puree
- 1/2 cup maple syrup or agave nectar
- 1/4 cup coconut oil, melted
- 1/2 teaspoon baking soda
- 1/2 teaspoon baking powder
- 1 teaspoon cinnamon
- 1/4 teaspoon nutmeg
- 1/4 teaspoon salt

Instructions

1. **Preheat the Oven:** Preheat your oven to 350°F (175°C) and grease a loaf pan.
2. **Mix Wet Ingredients:** In a bowl, combine the pumpkin puree, maple syrup, and melted coconut oil until well blended.
3. **Mix Dry Ingredients:** In another bowl, whisk together the flour, baking soda, baking powder, cinnamon, nutmeg, and salt.
4. **Combine Mixtures:** Gradually add the dry ingredients to the wet ingredients and mix until just combined.
5. **Pour into Loaf Pan:** Pour the batter into the greased loaf pan and smooth the top.
6. **Bake:** Bake for 50-60 minutes or until a toothpick inserted in the center comes out clean.
7. **Cool and Serve:** Allow to cool before slicing. Enjoy this moist pumpkin bread!

Millet Flour Banana Bread

Ingredients

- 1 1/2 cups millet flour
- 2 ripe bananas, mashed
- 1/2 cup maple syrup or honey
- 1/4 cup coconut oil, melted
- 2 large eggs
- 1 teaspoon baking powder
- 1/2 teaspoon baking soda
- 1/4 teaspoon salt
- 1 teaspoon vanilla extract

Instructions

1. **Preheat the Oven:** Preheat your oven to 350°F (175°C) and grease a loaf pan.
2. **Mix Wet Ingredients:** In a bowl, combine the mashed bananas, maple syrup (or honey), melted coconut oil, and eggs until smooth.
3. **Mix Dry Ingredients:** In another bowl, whisk together the millet flour, baking powder, baking soda, and salt.
4. **Combine Mixtures:** Gradually add the dry ingredients to the wet ingredients and mix until well combined.
5. **Pour into Loaf Pan:** Pour the batter into the prepared loaf pan and smooth the top.
6. **Bake:** Bake for 40-45 minutes or until a toothpick inserted in the center comes out clean.
7. **Cool and Serve:** Allow to cool before slicing. Enjoy this delicious banana bread!

Coconut Oil Chocolate Cake

Ingredients

- 1 3/4 cups all-purpose flour
- 3/4 cup cocoa powder
- 1 cup coconut sugar or brown sugar
- 1 teaspoon baking soda
- 1/2 teaspoon baking powder
- 1/4 teaspoon salt
- 1 cup almond milk or any dairy-free milk
- 1/2 cup coconut oil, melted
- 1 teaspoon vanilla extract
- 1 tablespoon apple cider vinegar

Instructions

1. **Preheat the Oven:** Preheat your oven to 350°F (175°C) and grease two 8-inch round cake pans.
2. **Mix Dry Ingredients:** In a bowl, whisk together the flour, cocoa powder, coconut sugar, baking soda, baking powder, and salt.
3. **Combine Wet Ingredients:** In another bowl, mix the almond milk, melted coconut oil, vanilla extract, and apple cider vinegar until smooth.
4. **Combine Mixtures:** Add the wet ingredients to the dry ingredients and stir until just combined.
5. **Divide and Bake:** Divide the batter evenly between the prepared cake pans and smooth the tops.
6. **Bake:** Bake for 25-30 minutes or until a toothpick inserted in the center comes out clean.
7. **Cool and Serve:** Allow to cool in the pans for a few minutes before transferring to a wire rack.

Peanut Butter and Jelly Cookies

Ingredients

- 1 cup natural peanut butter
- 1/2 cup coconut sugar
- 1/4 cup maple syrup or honey
- 1/2 teaspoon baking soda
- 1/4 teaspoon salt
- 1/2 cup jelly or jam of choice

Instructions

1. **Preheat the Oven:** Preheat your oven to 350°F (175°C) and line a baking sheet with parchment paper.
2. **Mix Ingredients:** In a bowl, combine the peanut butter, coconut sugar, maple syrup (or honey), baking soda, and salt until smooth.
3. **Shape Cookies:** Scoop tablespoon-sized portions of dough and place them on the prepared baking sheet, spacing them about 2 inches apart.
4. **Make Indentations:** Use your thumb or the back of a spoon to make an indentation in the center of each cookie. Fill with jelly or jam.
5. **Bake:** Bake for 10-12 minutes or until the edges are lightly golden.
6. **Cool and Serve:** Allow to cool on the baking sheet for a few minutes before transferring to a wire rack.

Flax Egg Pancakes

Ingredients

- 1 cup all-purpose flour
- 1 tablespoon flaxseed meal
- 1 cup almond milk or any dairy-free milk
- 1 tablespoon maple syrup or honey
- 1 teaspoon baking powder
- 1/4 teaspoon salt
- 1 tablespoon coconut oil, melted (for cooking)

Instructions

1. **Make Flax Egg:** In a small bowl, mix the flaxseed meal with 3 tablespoons of water. Let it sit for about 5 minutes until it thickens.
2. **Mix Dry Ingredients:** In a large bowl, whisk together the flour, baking powder, and salt.
3. **Combine Wet Ingredients:** Add the almond milk, maple syrup (or honey), and the prepared flax egg to the dry ingredients. Stir until combined.
4. **Heat Pan:** Heat a non-stick skillet over medium heat and add a small amount of coconut oil.
5. **Cook Pancakes:** Pour 1/4 cup of batter onto the skillet for each pancake. Cook until bubbles form on the surface, then flip and cook until golden brown on both sides.
6. **Serve:** Serve warm with your favorite toppings.

Enjoy making and savoring these delicious recipes!

Raw Vegan Cheesecake

Ingredients

- 1 cup raw cashews, soaked for at least 4 hours
- 1/2 cup coconut oil, melted
- 1/4 cup maple syrup or agave nectar
- 1/4 cup fresh lemon juice
- 1 teaspoon vanilla extract
- 1/4 teaspoon salt
- 1 cup mixed berries (for topping, optional)

Instructions

1. **Prepare the Crust:** In a food processor, blend 1 cup of dates and 1 cup of nuts until a sticky mixture forms. Press the mixture into the bottom of a springform pan.
2. **Make the Filling:** Drain and rinse the soaked cashews. In a blender, combine the cashews, melted coconut oil, maple syrup, lemon juice, vanilla extract, and salt. Blend until smooth and creamy.
3. **Assemble:** Pour the filling over the crust in the springform pan and smooth the top.
4. **Chill:** Refrigerate for at least 4 hours or until set.
5. **Serve:** Top with mixed berries before serving, if desired.

Chocolate Chip Chickpea Blondies

Ingredients

- 1 can (15 oz) chickpeas, drained and rinsed
- 1/2 cup almond butter or peanut butter
- 1/4 cup maple syrup
- 1 teaspoon vanilla extract
- 1/2 teaspoon baking powder
- 1/4 teaspoon salt
- 1/2 cup chocolate chips

Instructions

1. **Preheat the Oven:** Preheat your oven to 350°F (175°C) and grease an 8x8 inch baking pan.
2. **Blend Ingredients:** In a food processor, combine the chickpeas, almond butter, maple syrup, vanilla extract, baking powder, and salt. Blend until smooth.
3. **Fold in Chocolate Chips:** Transfer the mixture to a bowl and fold in the chocolate chips.
4. **Bake:** Spread the mixture evenly in the prepared baking pan and bake for 25-30 minutes.
5. **Cool and Serve:** Allow to cool before cutting into squares. Enjoy these blondies warm or at room temperature!

Cornmeal Muffins

Ingredients

- 1 cup cornmeal
- 1 cup all-purpose flour
- 1/4 cup sugar
- 1 tablespoon baking powder
- 1/2 teaspoon salt
- 1 cup almond milk or any dairy-free milk
- 1/4 cup coconut oil, melted
- 1 teaspoon vanilla extract

Instructions

1. **Preheat the Oven:** Preheat your oven to 400°F (200°C) and line a muffin tin with paper liners.
2. **Mix Dry Ingredients:** In a large bowl, combine the cornmeal, flour, sugar, baking powder, and salt.
3. **Combine Wet Ingredients:** In another bowl, whisk together the almond milk, melted coconut oil, and vanilla extract.
4. **Combine Mixtures:** Add the wet ingredients to the dry ingredients and stir until just combined.
5. **Fill Muffin Liners:** Pour the batter into the lined muffin cups, filling each about 2/3 full.
6. **Bake:** Bake for 15-20 minutes or until a toothpick inserted into the center comes out clean.
7. **Cool and Serve:** Allow to cool slightly before serving. Enjoy these delicious muffins warm!

Tapioca Flour Cookies

Ingredients

- 1 cup tapioca flour
- 1/2 cup coconut sugar
- 1/4 cup coconut oil, melted
- 1/4 cup almond milk or any dairy-free milk
- 1 teaspoon vanilla extract
- 1/2 teaspoon baking powder
- 1/4 teaspoon salt

Instructions

1. **Preheat the Oven:** Preheat your oven to 350°F (175°C) and line a baking sheet with parchment paper.
2. **Mix Wet Ingredients:** In a bowl, mix the melted coconut oil, coconut sugar, almond milk, and vanilla extract until well combined.
3. **Combine Dry Ingredients:** In another bowl, whisk together the tapioca flour, baking powder, and salt.
4. **Combine Mixtures:** Gradually add the dry ingredients to the wet ingredients and mix until a dough forms.
5. **Shape Cookies:** Scoop tablespoon-sized portions of dough and place them on the prepared baking sheet.
6. **Bake:** Bake for 10-12 minutes or until lightly golden.
7. **Cool and Serve:** Allow to cool before transferring to a wire rack.

Coconut Flour Snickerdoodles

Ingredients

- 1/2 cup coconut flour
- 1/2 teaspoon baking soda
- 1/4 teaspoon salt
- 1/4 cup coconut oil, melted
- 1/4 cup coconut sugar
- 1/4 cup maple syrup or honey
- 1 teaspoon vanilla extract
- 1 tablespoon cinnamon (for coating)

Instructions

1. **Preheat the Oven:** Preheat your oven to 350°F (175°C) and line a baking sheet with parchment paper.
2. **Mix Dry Ingredients:** In a bowl, whisk together the coconut flour, baking soda, and salt.
3. **Combine Wet Ingredients:** In another bowl, mix the melted coconut oil, coconut sugar, maple syrup (or honey), and vanilla extract until smooth.
4. **Combine Mixtures:** Add the dry ingredients to the wet ingredients and mix until well combined.
5. **Shape Cookies:** Scoop tablespoon-sized portions of dough, roll them into balls, and roll in the cinnamon.
6. **Bake:** Place on the prepared baking sheet and bake for 10-12 minutes or until lightly golden.
7. **Cool and Serve:** Allow to cool before transferring to a wire rack.

Almond Milk Scones

Ingredients

- 2 cups all-purpose flour
- 1/4 cup coconut sugar
- 1 tablespoon baking powder
- 1/2 teaspoon salt
- 1/4 cup coconut oil, solid
- 3/4 cup almond milk or any dairy-free milk
- 1 teaspoon vanilla extract

Instructions

1. **Preheat the Oven:** Preheat your oven to 375°F (190°C) and line a baking sheet with parchment paper.
2. **Mix Dry Ingredients:** In a large bowl, whisk together the flour, coconut sugar, baking powder, and salt.
3. **Cut in Coconut Oil:** Add the solid coconut oil and cut it into the flour mixture until it resembles coarse crumbs.
4. **Combine Wet Ingredients:** In another bowl, combine the almond milk and vanilla extract.
5. **Combine Mixtures:** Pour the wet ingredients into the dry ingredients and stir until just combined.
6. **Shape Scones:** Turn the dough onto a floured surface and gently knead. Pat into a circle about 1-inch thick and cut into wedges.
7. **Bake:** Place on the prepared baking sheet and bake for 15-20 minutes or until lightly golden.
8. **Cool and Serve:** Allow to cool slightly before serving. Enjoy these delightful scones!

Enjoy preparing and tasting these delicious recipes!

Lentil Flour Brownies

Ingredients

- 1 cup lentil flour
- 1/2 cup cocoa powder
- 1/2 cup maple syrup or honey
- 1/4 cup coconut oil, melted
- 1/4 cup almond milk or any dairy-free milk
- 1 teaspoon vanilla extract
- 1/2 teaspoon baking powder
- 1/4 teaspoon salt
- 1/2 cup chocolate chips (optional)

Instructions

1. **Preheat the Oven:** Preheat your oven to 350°F (175°C) and grease an 8x8 inch baking pan.
2. **Mix Dry Ingredients:** In a bowl, combine lentil flour, cocoa powder, baking powder, and salt.
3. **Mix Wet Ingredients:** In another bowl, mix the maple syrup, melted coconut oil, almond milk, and vanilla extract until smooth.
4. **Combine Mixtures:** Add the wet ingredients to the dry ingredients and mix until well combined. Fold in chocolate chips if using.
5. **Bake:** Pour the batter into the prepared baking pan and bake for 20-25 minutes.
6. **Cool and Serve:** Allow to cool before cutting into squares. Enjoy!

Sweet Potato Muffins with Oat Flour

Ingredients

- 1 cup oat flour
- 1 cup mashed sweet potatoes (cooked)
- 1/4 cup maple syrup
- 1/4 cup coconut oil, melted
- 1/2 teaspoon baking powder
- 1/2 teaspoon baking soda
- 1/4 teaspoon salt
- 1 teaspoon cinnamon
- 1/2 cup walnuts or pecans (optional)

Instructions

1. **Preheat the Oven:** Preheat your oven to 375°F (190°C) and line a muffin tin with paper liners.
2. **Mix Dry Ingredients:** In a bowl, whisk together oat flour, baking powder, baking soda, salt, and cinnamon.
3. **Mix Wet Ingredients:** In another bowl, combine mashed sweet potatoes, maple syrup, and melted coconut oil.
4. **Combine Mixtures:** Add the wet ingredients to the dry ingredients and mix until just combined. Fold in nuts if using.
5. **Fill Muffin Liners:** Divide the batter among the muffin cups.
6. **Bake:** Bake for 20-25 minutes or until a toothpick comes out clean.
7. **Cool and Serve:** Allow to cool slightly before serving.

Gluten-Free Chocolate Torte

Ingredients

- 1 cup almond flour
- 1/2 cup cocoa powder
- 1/2 cup maple syrup or agave nectar
- 1/4 cup coconut oil, melted
- 4 large eggs
- 1 teaspoon vanilla extract
- 1/2 teaspoon baking powder
- 1/4 teaspoon salt

Instructions

1. **Preheat the Oven:** Preheat your oven to 350°F (175°C) and grease an 8-inch round cake pan.
2. **Mix Ingredients:** In a large bowl, combine almond flour, cocoa powder, baking powder, and salt. In another bowl, whisk together eggs, maple syrup, melted coconut oil, and vanilla extract.
3. **Combine Mixtures:** Pour the wet ingredients into the dry ingredients and mix until smooth.
4. **Bake:** Pour the batter into the prepared cake pan and bake for 25-30 minutes.
5. **Cool and Serve:** Allow to cool before serving. Dust with cocoa powder or serve with fresh berries.

Carob Flour Cookies

Ingredients

- 1 cup carob flour
- 1/2 cup almond butter or peanut butter
- 1/4 cup coconut sugar
- 1/4 cup maple syrup
- 1 teaspoon vanilla extract
- 1/2 teaspoon baking soda
- 1/4 teaspoon salt

Instructions

1. **Preheat the Oven:** Preheat your oven to 350°F (175°C) and line a baking sheet with parchment paper.
2. **Mix Wet Ingredients:** In a bowl, mix almond butter, coconut sugar, maple syrup, and vanilla extract until smooth.
3. **Mix Dry Ingredients:** In another bowl, combine carob flour, baking soda, and salt.
4. **Combine Mixtures:** Add the dry ingredients to the wet ingredients and mix until well combined.
5. **Shape Cookies:** Scoop tablespoon-sized portions of dough and place them on the baking sheet.
6. **Bake:** Bake for 10-12 minutes or until slightly golden.
7. **Cool and Serve:** Allow to cool before transferring to a wire rack.

Green Banana Flour Pancakes

Ingredients

- 1 cup green banana flour
- 1 cup almond milk or any dairy-free milk
- 2 tablespoons coconut oil, melted
- 1 tablespoon maple syrup (optional)
- 1 teaspoon baking powder
- 1/4 teaspoon salt

Instructions

1. **Mix Ingredients:** In a bowl, combine green banana flour, baking powder, and salt. In another bowl, mix almond milk, melted coconut oil, and maple syrup.
2. **Combine Mixtures:** Pour the wet ingredients into the dry ingredients and mix until smooth.
3. **Cook Pancakes:** Heat a non-stick skillet over medium heat. Pour 1/4 cup of batter for each pancake and cook until bubbles form, then flip and cook until golden.
4. **Serve:** Serve warm with your favorite toppings.

Vegan Coconut Macaroons

Ingredients

- 2 cups shredded unsweetened coconut
- 1/2 cup almond flour
- 1/4 cup maple syrup
- 1/4 cup coconut oil, melted
- 1 teaspoon vanilla extract
- 1/4 teaspoon salt

Instructions

1. **Preheat the Oven:** Preheat your oven to 350°F (175°C) and line a baking sheet with parchment paper.
2. **Mix Ingredients:** In a bowl, combine shredded coconut, almond flour, maple syrup, melted coconut oil, vanilla extract, and salt. Mix until well combined.
3. **Shape Macaroons:** Use a tablespoon to scoop the mixture and shape it into small mounds on the prepared baking sheet.
4. **Bake:** Bake for 15-20 minutes or until lightly golden.
5. **Cool and Serve:** Allow to cool before serving. Enjoy these delicious treats!

Oat and Honey Granola Bars

Ingredients

- 2 cups rolled oats
- 1/2 cup almond butter or peanut butter
- 1/2 cup honey or maple syrup
- 1/4 cup almond flour
- 1/4 cup chopped nuts or seeds (optional)
- 1/4 cup dried fruit (optional)
- 1 teaspoon vanilla extract
- 1/2 teaspoon salt

Instructions

1. **Preheat the Oven:** Preheat your oven to 350°F (175°C) and line an 8x8 inch baking pan with parchment paper.
2. **Mix Ingredients:** In a large bowl, combine rolled oats, almond butter, honey, almond flour, nuts or seeds, dried fruit, vanilla extract, and salt. Mix until well combined.
3. **Press Mixture:** Pour the mixture into the prepared baking pan and press down firmly.
4. **Bake:** Bake for 20-25 minutes or until golden.
5. **Cool and Cut:** Allow to cool completely before cutting into bars. Enjoy!

Quinoa Chocolate Chip Cookies

Ingredients

- 1 cup cooked quinoa
- 1/2 cup almond flour
- 1/4 cup coconut oil, melted
- 1/4 cup maple syrup or honey
- 1 teaspoon vanilla extract
- 1/2 teaspoon baking powder
- 1/4 teaspoon salt
- 1/2 cup chocolate chips

Instructions

1. **Preheat the Oven:** Preheat your oven to 350°F (175°C) and line a baking sheet with parchment paper.
2. **Mix Ingredients:** In a bowl, combine cooked quinoa, almond flour, melted coconut oil, maple syrup, vanilla extract, baking powder, and salt. Mix until smooth. Fold in chocolate chips.
3. **Shape Cookies:** Scoop tablespoon-sized portions of dough and place them on the baking sheet.
4. **Bake:** Bake for 10-12 minutes or until lightly golden.
5. **Cool and Serve:** Allow to cool before transferring to a wire rack.

Enjoy making and savoring these delicious recipes!

Brown Rice Flour Cookies

Ingredients

- 1 cup brown rice flour
- 1/2 cup coconut sugar
- 1/4 cup coconut oil, melted
- 1/4 cup maple syrup
- 1 teaspoon vanilla extract
- 1/2 teaspoon baking soda
- 1/4 teaspoon salt
- 1/2 cup chocolate chips (optional)

Instructions

1. **Preheat the Oven:** Preheat your oven to 350°F (175°C) and line a baking sheet with parchment paper.
2. **Mix Dry Ingredients:** In a bowl, combine brown rice flour, baking soda, and salt.
3. **Mix Wet Ingredients:** In another bowl, whisk together melted coconut oil, coconut sugar, maple syrup, and vanilla extract until smooth.
4. **Combine Mixtures:** Add the wet ingredients to the dry ingredients and mix until well combined. Fold in chocolate chips if using.
5. **Shape Cookies:** Scoop tablespoon-sized portions of dough and place them on the prepared baking sheet.
6. **Bake:** Bake for 10-12 minutes or until the edges are golden.
7. **Cool and Serve:** Allow to cool before transferring to a wire rack.

Acorn Flour Pancakes

Ingredients

- 1 cup acorn flour
- 1 cup almond milk or any dairy-free milk
- 2 tablespoons maple syrup
- 1 tablespoon coconut oil, melted
- 1 teaspoon baking powder
- 1/4 teaspoon salt

Instructions

1. **Mix Dry Ingredients:** In a bowl, combine acorn flour, baking powder, and salt.
2. **Mix Wet Ingredients:** In another bowl, mix almond milk, maple syrup, and melted coconut oil.
3. **Combine Mixtures:** Pour the wet ingredients into the dry ingredients and mix until smooth.
4. **Cook Pancakes:** Heat a non-stick skillet over medium heat. Pour 1/4 cup of batter for each pancake and cook until bubbles form, then flip and cook until golden.
5. **Serve:** Serve warm with your favorite toppings.

Vegan Blueberry Muffins

Ingredients

- 1 cup whole wheat flour
- 1/2 cup almond milk
- 1/4 cup maple syrup
- 1/4 cup coconut oil, melted
- 1 teaspoon vanilla extract
- 1 teaspoon baking powder
- 1/2 teaspoon baking soda
- 1/4 teaspoon salt
- 1 cup fresh or frozen blueberries

Instructions

1. **Preheat the Oven:** Preheat your oven to 350°F (175°C) and line a muffin tin with paper liners.
2. **Mix Dry Ingredients:** In a bowl, combine whole wheat flour, baking powder, baking soda, and salt.
3. **Mix Wet Ingredients:** In another bowl, whisk together almond milk, maple syrup, melted coconut oil, and vanilla extract.
4. **Combine Mixtures:** Add the wet ingredients to the dry ingredients and mix until just combined. Gently fold in blueberries.
5. **Fill Muffin Liners:** Divide the batter among the muffin cups.
6. **Bake:** Bake for 18-20 minutes or until a toothpick comes out clean.
7. **Cool and Serve:** Allow to cool slightly before serving.

Chocolate Avocado Cake

Ingredients

- 1 ripe avocado, mashed
- 1 cup almond flour
- 1/2 cup cocoa powder
- 1/2 cup maple syrup or agave nectar
- 1/4 cup coconut oil, melted
- 4 large eggs
- 1 teaspoon vanilla extract
- 1 teaspoon baking soda
- 1/4 teaspoon salt

Instructions

1. **Preheat the Oven:** Preheat your oven to 350°F (175°C) and grease an 8-inch round cake pan.
2. **Mix Ingredients:** In a large bowl, combine mashed avocado, almond flour, cocoa powder, baking soda, and salt. In another bowl, whisk together eggs, maple syrup, melted coconut oil, and vanilla extract.
3. **Combine Mixtures:** Pour the wet ingredients into the dry ingredients and mix until smooth.
4. **Bake:** Pour the batter into the prepared cake pan and bake for 25-30 minutes.
5. **Cool and Serve:** Allow to cool before serving. Dust with cocoa powder or serve with fresh berries.

Enjoy these delightful recipes!